Managing Your Hindu Wedding in North America: The Day Before and THE Day!

A Guide for Couples, their Families and Priest

by

Dr. A.V. Srinivasan

Periplus Line LLC

Copyright © 2017 by Periplus Line LLC,
A.V. Srinivasan

ISBN 10: 0-9785443-8-2
ISBN 13: 978-0-978-5443-8-6

First Edition

All rights reserved. No part of this book may be reproduced or utilized in any form or by any means, electronic or mechanical, including photocopying, recording, or by any information storage or retrieval system, without permission in writing from the Publisher.

Inquiries should be addressed to the Publisher:
Periplus Line LLC
Attention: Permissions Department
P.O. Box 56, East Glastonbury, CT 06025-0056 U.S.A.
www.periplusbooks.com

Srinivasan, A. V.
    Managing Your Hindu Wedding in North America: The Day Before and THE Day!
    A Guide to Couples, their Families and Priest

In English, with Sanskrit citations; glossary.

1. Marriage service (Hinduism) --- Preparation guide. 2. Marriage customs and rites --- Hindu. 3. Wedding rehearsal.

Printed in the United States of America

Managing Your Hindu Wedding in North America: The Day Before and THE Day!

by Dr. A.V. Srinivasan*

This book, ***Managing your Hindu Wedding in North America: The Day Before and THE Day***, serves as a guide to couples, their families and priest. An audio book and an ebook edition are also available.

To the couples, I say Congratulations! Your very special day is here at last. The magic of love that brought you two together will now be formalized through a traditional wedding ceremony. You are about to celebrate your heritage. You both need to know the phrase भार्या दैव कतः सखा which means "A wife is a God-given friend". The friendship element is central to your relationship for the rest of your life. Never forget that.

The Months Before: The Preparation

You have worked together for months planning: consulting friends, researching, discussing with both parents, maybe even arguing pros and cons, who should be invited, how long the ceremony should be, booking the venue, DJ, flowers, photographers, hair dressers, choosing dresses to wear at the Sangeet, the ceremony and reception, bride's maids, selecting music, performers, sangeet and mehandi events the day before, type of food to be served, the caterer, the mantap, drinks, reception, dance, honeymoon, getting invitations printed, envelopes addressed and mailed and a host of major and minor details with the sole purpose of enjoying the next couple of days you have been dreaming to set the stage for an exciting married life. You prepared a time line on an excel sheet, emailed the wedding coordinator, friends and relatives who will help to make the two days special. You have proven to be the very model of efficiency indeed. All of that is behind you now. And you are anxious but satisfied that everything has been taken care of and all will go as planned. Perhaps! It depends!

Let me brief you about the one, the most critical and central element of the entire effort–the ceremony. It undoubtedly gets attention–but almost always less than it ought to receive. As a result the experience can be frustrating. You can avoid that if and only if you do, in your heart of hearts, believe that the most important element is The Ceremony. No amount of emails, spread sheets, colorful invitations can compensate for the most sacred part of the entire event if there is not an understanding of the various steps you will take during that critical hour. Trust me. It is a matter of self respect and discipline. In our format we have been successful in integrating joy and discipline. Recall your impressions of weddings of some of your friends you may have attended at a church or synagogue. Recall the hour inside that church with the audience engaged with the ceremony: The quiet, the solemnity, the dignity, the joy would have been evident. That is self respect, that is respect for the tradition and that is discipline.

The Months Before: The Preparation | 5

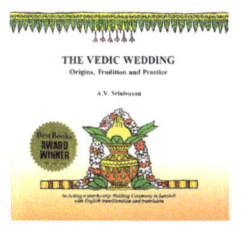

A Hindu wedding is based on the Vedas–specifically the Rg Veda where a detailed description is given of the wedding of Sūryā, daughter of the Sun god Sūrya. I discuss this in great detail in my book: *The Vedic Wedding: Origins, Tradition and Practice*. The Vedic base is a treasure we have inherited from our ancestors and it deserves respect and reverence.

Furthermore the mantras are meaningful, beautiful, pleasant, deep and inspiring when they are chanted with proper volume and intonation. You need to read, understand and pay attention to the meaning of the mantras you will be hearing and also repeating after the priest when asked. Please do not skip this step.

The Officiant/Priest and the Program

I strongly urge couples to engage a knowledgable priest to perform the ceremonies and study the ceremonial steps and develop an understanding of the rich traditions of your family. Otherwise it is truly a waste of time. This is not to discourage you but in fact to encourage you and urge you to go a little deeper so you can enjoy the hour-long experience of the Vedic-based format I have developed. This format preserves all the essential elements of the Vedic ceremony.

You need to select a priest who can communicate with and engage the audience throughout the hour. You should provide the priest family data which includes *gotras* and names of the lineages: greatgrandfather, grandfather and father from both families. These will be chanted during Pravara to proclaim the familes that are coming together to bless the union.

The priest's role is crucial during the hour. A single quote from an uncle of the groom, a Hindu, at a wedding I performed should convince you of the enjoyment that can come out of a well conducted Vedic ceremony: "The wedding was like watching a symphony" said the man after the ceremony.

With that brief background, let me set the stage for a series of steps you need to note and take on the day before at the rehearsal so that the ceremony next day will go smoothly like a "symphony". Your day should be special and it can be. Remember 3 phrases: (1) Attention to detail, (2) Attention to detail and(3) Attention to detail!

When once the wedding program is in place after meeting, consulting and finalizing with the assistance of your priest and printing the program at least a couple of weeks before the wedding day, it should be frozen. The tendency to add a last minute item or two can be avoided if the principals (the couple, both parents, uncles, aunts, friends, ...) involve themselves in the planning stage. And, by all means discuss all the steps and their implications and spatial arrangements at the mantap with the priest. Every step needs to be supported by appropriate mantras so it is unfair to you if the added steps do not receive the same attention. Make sure an aunt or an uncle visiting from India doesn't ask the night before: " Where is ...? " referring to a step! That may be a legitimate question, and one way to avoid such last minute dilemmas is to include them in the planning process.

The Months Before: The Preparation | 7

When you are looking for a priest make sure to listen to some of the chants to know if the intonations, sound clarity and volume are pleasant, inspiring and soothing to the mind.

The Day Before: The Rehearsal

Rehearsal for a Hindu wedding? Never heard of! But our plan and format demand it. In fact I refuse to perform a Hindu wedding without a rehearsal. I impress upon the families the importance of it and it works well. A good rehearsal results in a satisfying experience all around. But it is not a tradition and so some families don't take it seriously and try to get it over with by sandwiching it between hair appointments, airport runs to pick up relatives, sangeet, photographs etc. etc. The result is obvious and the confusion is visible at the ceremony. This lack of discipline and organization are precisely what puts off the audience and their attention is gone. I have been particularly fortunate in insisting on it and that results in pin-drop silence and undivided attention during the crucial ceremony hour of the "symphony!"

At the rehearsal (Note hand gestures)

You need a knowledgeable "director" to keep track of the flow of the ceremonial steps and provide cues. At first glance one wonders about the need for stage direction in a religious ceremony. After all it is not drama. Upon some reflection, however, it should be clear that in a sense it IS drama, a real life one in fact, where the principals and helpers have specified roles that they need to "play" without missing a beat so that the series of steps do indeed blend together to reflect the meaning and symbolism of the culture and tradition of the families. Much time and money have been invested for many months by the couple and their families. Friends and relatives arrive at the ceremony with great expectation and excitement to watch the couple on their very special day.

At the wedding

For these reasons, it is important to designate one individual as the director whose primary responsibility is to make sure that everyone and everything is in place as discussed during the weeks of planning and finalized at the rehearsal.

While the role of a wedding planner/coordinator covers the preparations in terms of locating and booking the venue, photographer, videographer, selection of clothes, gifts, invitations, music and related activities up to and surrounding the ceremony itself, the role of the director covers the central event. The director may be a knowledgeable friend or relative. He or she should be familiar with the entire ceremony. It is a given that the director and the coordinator should attend the rehearsal and be familiar with the geographical setting of the wedding site in order to visualize the flow of all the steps both in space and time. The goal is a smooth flow of steps at the ceremony. This is possible with a knowledgeable or experienced director.

The principals required at the rehearsal (depending upon the final program elements)

- Wedding coordinator (usually a staff member from the hotel or venue chosen by the couple)
- Ceremony Coordinator. I have been calling that person a Director who is usually an associate of the priest or priest-in-training who has full knowledge of the ceremonial steps and directs those family members or friends assigned to do specific tasks when cued as the ceremony progresses. For the sake of simplicity let us call this individual a director. This director could be a family member as long he/she is familiar with all the steps and knows how/when to cue. We will show some examples when we discuss cues later
- Bride, groom, and their parents and/or stand-ins
- Bride's entourage (Example: at least five young women from among the bride's siblings, uncles, aunts etc. and friends)
- Bridegroom's "best men" (Example: at least five young men who will assist as discussed and identified during the rehearsal)
- Bride's brother(s) to assist at Mangal Phera (also called Laja Homa)
- Groom's sister to assist while the *mangalasutra* is being tied
- Five married ladies from the bride's family who will be in the processional to greet the bridegroom
- Fire managers (two selected from the "best men")
- Garland bearers (one from each side), ring bearers
- A young boy or girl to collect water poured down during Kanyadanam
- Antarpat bearers (two selected from the "best men")
- Manager of *mangalasutra* blessing and *akshata* distribution (one selected from the five ladies above)

12 | Managing Your Hindu Wedding in North America

- Manager of sound/music/microphones (DJ)
- Manager of pictures/videos
- Ushers (selected from the "best men" and/or bride's family)
- Manager of the mantap: arrangements, arrivals/departures
- Hall manager to direct, control entry and exit doors, lighting, heat sensors

At the Rehearsal: Note the arrangement of materials on tables. The word Panchapatra shown below in the schematic refers to traditional 5 cups used in worships.

Note: At the wedding, the tables may be set just outside the mantap to save space on the mantap. The positioning of the bride's family and the groom's family shown below is optional.

The Day Before: The Rehearsal

Mantap Arrangement Schematic
Size about 20' x 16' generally facing east
Steps from both sides, firm and easy to use

```
┌─────────────────────────────────────────────────────┐
│  ┌─────────────────────────┐                        │
│  │ Plates: fruits, flowers,│                        │
│  │   incense, mangalyam,   │  ┌──────────────────┐  │
│  │  madhuparkam, kalasha,  │  │ Havan samagris,  │  │
│  │  coconut, antarpat sheet,│  │ ghee, camphor,   │  │
│  │   kanyadanam vessels.   │  │ puffed rice,     │  │
│  └─────────────────────────┘  │ matches          │  │
│                               └──────────────────┘  │
│                                                     │
│       Bride's Family              Groom's Family    │
│                      ┌──────────┐                   │
│                      │Agnikunda │                   │
│                      │placed and│                   │
│                      │ removed  │                   │
│                      │upon cue  │                   │
│    ╭─────────╮       └──────────┘  ┌─────────────┐  │
│   ╱ Panchapatra╲                   │ Rings       │  │
│  │  Uddharana   │                  │ Stone slab  │  │
│  │  Akshata     │                  │ Toe Rings   │  │
│   ╲ Petals    ╱                    │ Napkins     │  │
│    ╰─────────╯                     └─────────────┘  │
└─────────────────────────────────────────────────────┘
```

Audience

Rehearsal Plan

1. Set a time when ALL of the above can be present, preferably the afternoon before the wedding
2. Introductions of principals by either the bride or the groom or the parents
3. Discuss the barāt; arrival on horse, car or foot, time to begin and end
4. Determine locations and times (place where the bridegroom is to be met, place where the bride will start her processional, length of time needed to reach the mantap, bride's entourage)
5. Set the time when the ceremony begins *
6. Instruct the groom's family to stand to the left of the priest facing the audience and the bride's family to the right. This is NOT a rigid requirement
7. Discussion of what will take place step-by-step by the priest/officiant

8. Make sure the venue has no objection to building a fire for the homas
9. Roles and responsibilities outlined: Director writes down names to cue
10. Meet at the site and walk through the main steps, discuss and practice "difficult" steps, (Invocation of sacred rivers, Kanyadanam, tying of the mangalasutra, pherās, Saptapadi), and practice lighting fire
11. Assemble materials
12. Discuss the role of the ceremony director (cues, communication, placement and movement of principals)
13. Understand when the ceremony begins and ends **
14. Prescribe that the helpers will be at the mantap at least one hour before the ceremony is scheduled to begin. Assign the materials they each need to bring and assemble at the mantap. See the materials list.
15. Designate the wedding coordinator to call each helper early in the morning to be sure they will be there. And you need to name substitutes, just in case. Let the wedding coordinator be in charge of this task to manage last minute no-shows.
16. Decide if the audience can be seated before or immediately after the Barāt. Let the DJ make appropriate announcements.

* The ceremony officially begins when the bride's party (priest, bride's parents, five ladies and any other group of elders and friends from the bride's side) assembles at and leaves the mantap and proceeds to receive the bridegroom and his party at the decorated gate or other designated location. This processional must arrive a few seconds earlier and wait for the arrival of the bridegroom's party.

** The ceremony ends when the officiator announces the couple as Mr. & Mrs. .... and the couple descends from the mantap to seek the blessings of elders from both families, prior to walking down the aisle.

Wedding Materials List

- **akshata** (yellow turmeric-tinted raw rice), 1 lb.
- **kumkum** (red powder), 2 tablespoons.
- **haldi** (turmeric), 4 tablespoons.
- **agarbattis, small deepa with wick, matches**.
- **fruits and flowers**, 3 to 5 kinds; loose petals, plate of sweets, 1 decorated coconut; the above can all be arranged on 3 or 4 plates.
- **perfume sprinkler** (optional).
- **garlands (minimum 2)**, for bride and groom; more if needed by family tradition at Swagatam or Milni if others in the families need to be garlanded.
- **water** in 1 pitcher or kalasha; extra bowl or smaller kalasha and one ceremonial spoon (uddharana); large bowl or plate
- **coconut lightly coated with turmeric**, for Kanyadanam.
- **paper towels or napkins** to wipe hands as needed
- **glass mantles or cover** protection for deepas/candles used in outdoor ceremonies (or use of battery-assisted substitutes)
- **mangalasutra (necklace), rings, sindhur, toe rings** (optional, as dictated by family practice) on a decorative plate
- **a large sheet or a saree for Antarpat** (optional; if it is the family tradition)
- **a slab or rock for Ashmarohana** (optional; if it is the family tradition)

- **Materials for Homas/ Fire Rituals** (Do not bring huge amounts. Offerings are symbolic; for example no more than a cup of havan samagri would be more than adequate)
    - **havan kund** or equivalent metal or metal-lined grille, about 18" x 18"

- **small steady stool/table**, metal or tile-topped.
- **bricks** or tiles; aluminum foil
- **dry sticks; paper; 2 fire-starter cakes**
- **matchsticks or fire lighter**; **camphor**; **dry coconut pieces**
- **havan samagri** in a bowl; a cup of **akshata**; on tray
- **small jar of ghee**, with **spoon**
- **puffed/parched rice** (laja) in 4 small cups
- **sand** in bucket for fire control, discreetly located at rear

A few illustrations shown below may be helpful in planning to assemble and organize a variety of requirements:

One of the plates taken to Milni

Fruits, petals, water

Rangoli floor decoration

Agni Kunda

Samagris: Note paper towel

Deepas

Wedding Materials List | 19

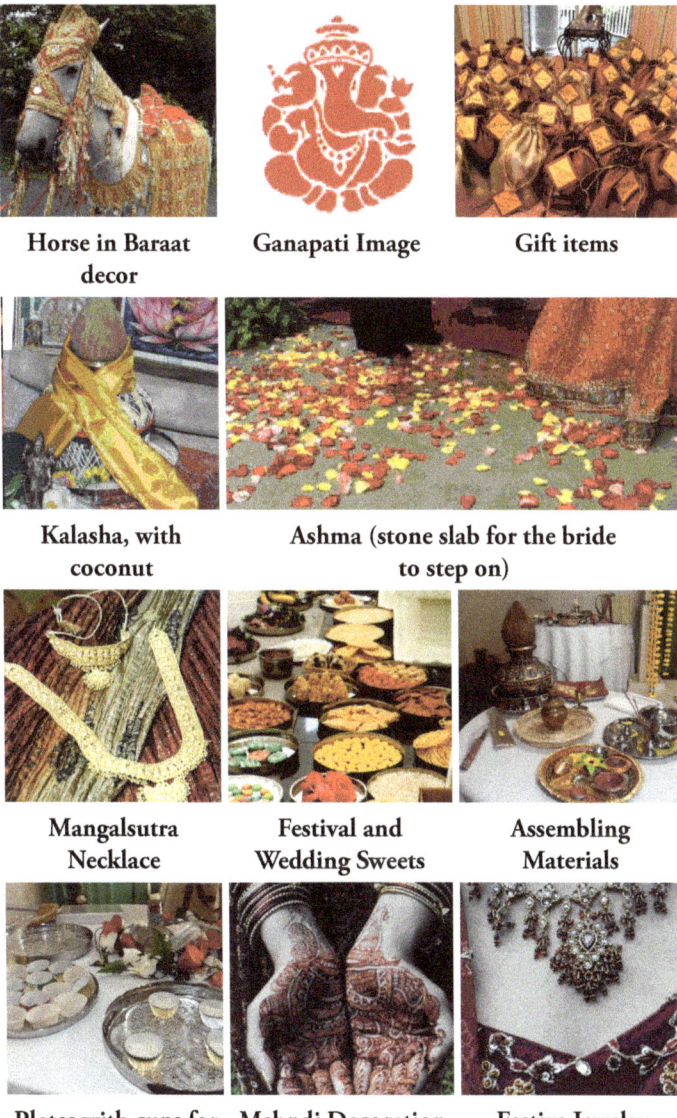

Horse in Baraat decor

Ganapati Image

Gift items

Kalasha, with coconut

Ashma (stone slab for the bride to step on)

Mangalsutra Necklace

Festival and Wedding Sweets

Assembling Materials

Plates with cups for havan samagris

Mehndi Decoration

Festive Jewelry

THE DAY

Follow these steps to the letter and you can have a great ceremony:

1. The wedding coordinator calls the assigned helpers to make sure they will be at the mantap at the hour agreed on.
2. Helpers will bring all the materials from a central or different locations to the mantap.
3. Arrange tables on both sides of the mantap for easy access by the helpers and priest.
4. Assemble one small plate for the priest to carry with akshata, flower petals, a water-filled ceremonial bowl with *uddharana*
5. Assemble 5 plates with fruits, flowers, garland, kalasha, coconut, agarbatti (lit), sweets, deepa (lamp) with haldi and kumkum.
6. Assemble havan samagri, akshata, puffed rice and ghee, all on one plate and set it aside for easy access
7. Keep in order of use items needed for the ceremony
8. Place the agni-kunda, materials ready for lighting, and a 24" stool (the kunda can be set on this table) to the side ready to be lit when the fire manager receives a cue from the director. The sand should also be kept nearby for extinguishing the fire when it is removed from the mantap after *saptapadi*.
9. After all needed materials have been arranged ready to use, put away all boxes out of sight.
10. And you are all set! Go and do it and enjoy!

Outline for the Wedding Ceremony

Sometimes I say that there are a billion plus Hindus around the world and there could be as many types of weddings under the banner of Hindu wedding. The extent of variation is dictated by family traditions. In modern times in North America I emphasize retaining family traditions and leave the choice of steps to the couple and their families but at the same time discuss the Vedic basis which is rooted in friendship more than anything else. And it works out well. Based on Vedic sources, a desired framework of space and time, and family tradition, the following basic steps meet most needs:

Basic Steps

- Swagat/ Swagatam or Milni: The meeting and greeting of both families.
- Vara Puja: Dialogue between the bride's father and the groom.
- Jayamala/Jai Mala: Exchange of garlands.
- Pravara: Announcement of lineage.
- Kanyadanam: Giving away the bride.
- Mangalyadharanam: Tying the mangalasutra.
- Agni/Homas: Fire rituals.
- Mangal Phera: Circling the fire.
- Saptapadi: Seven steps.
- Ashirvadam: Blessings.

A final program can be developed around this framework. Some steps can be omitted, and some added, e.g. vows, ring exchange, etc. See the full list and discussion of additional rites in my book ***The Vedic Wedding: Origins, Tradition and Practice***.

Cueing

Study the steps discussed just now carefully and note that for these events to flow smoothly without missing a beat, certain individuals identified at the rehearsal need to be alerted by the ceremony director watching the progress quietly outside the mantap and sending silent signals (by gesture, nodding, etc.) so that they do their allotted tasks promptly. As an example, just as Kanyadanam is taking place, the director signals a lady identified the night before at the rehearsal to take the previously assembled mangalasutra plate and have the *māngalyam* blessed by elders from both families seated in the front row. Another example is when the Mangalyadharanam is taking place the fire manager is cued to get ready to light the fire and bring it on to the mantap just as the priest completes the Mangalyadharanam ceremony. Plan these cues the night before and inform those assigned for particular tasks at each step to be on the alert. Without these cues time is wasted and the audience may get restless. Let me list the precise moments when cues are given:

1. Cue the bride's family assembled to meet and greet the groom and his family as the Barat is about to conclude
2. Cue the wedding coordinator to signal the bride's entourage to process as soon as the dialog between the bride's father and groom ends. The appropriate mantra is *"yathā jnānam karavāñi"* uttered by the groom. This response from the groom, it may be noted, means "I shall do so to the best of my knowledge" and is in answer to the priest's charge asking the groom to perform the wedding rites according to prescribed *shāstrās*.
3. Cue the child selected to hold the plate to collect water poured over the coconut during Kanyadanam
4. Cue the lady tasked with getting the *māngalyam* blessed as the Kanyadanam is taking place
5. Cue the fire manager to light the fire as the priest blesses the bride with the mantra *"yathendrñi mahendrasya ... "*)
6. Cue the bride's brother to keep the bowl of parched rice (*lāja*) to offer to the bride and groom as they begin the Mangal Phera (or Laja Homa)
7. Cue the fire manager to remove the agni kunda from the mantap as soon as *saptapadi* is over.

Basic Steps with Description

- **Preliminary rites** to the wedding ceremony can include one or more of the following: **Ganesh Puja**, **Gauri Puja**, **Yajnopavitam** ceremonies may take place the night before.

- **Swagat/ Swagatam or Milni**: The meeting and greeting of both families.

On the day of wedding, Sehra Bandi (turban tying), or a *kashiyātra* ceremony for the groom may be included. There may also be a long or an abbreviated **Barāt** (joyous arrival of the groom, his family and friends with dancing and music riding, for example, a horse, a cart, a car, or on foot.)

At the *swāgatam* ceremony as the Barāt concludes, the groom and his entourage are greeted, at a predetermined location (the door or gateway to the venue), by the priest, bride's parents, siblings, and other relatives, including at least five married ladies carrying plates of fruits, flowers, deepa (lamp), dhoopa (incense), garland for the groom and new clothing if desired.

The priest blesses the groom, and prays for an obstacle-free ceremony. I begin by blessing the groom by sprinkling *akshata* as he bends his head in reverence and chant shlokas in praise of Ganapati and Vishnu.

The bride's father garlands him, and other relatives on the bride's side may, based on a previous plan, garland corresponding relatives on the groom's side. The bride's mother is instructed to perform an *arati*, anointing the groom with a *tilak*, and *akshata* (turmeric-tinted raw rice), and sprinkling perfumed water. The groom may receive a sweet or sweet drink at this time from the bride's parent, or later from the bride.

The groom is then escorted by the priest and both the families to the mantap.

Overview

In the format I have developed I give the assembled guests and families a five minute overview of the whole program emphasizing their active participation and urging them to stay alert as I ask for their permission along the way at different intervals and ask that they respond with a single word in Sanskrit: *Tathāstu* to indicate their approvals.

Vedic Chants

Subsequent to the overview I begin with Vedic chants and invoke the sacred rivers of India. In my format I have included invocation of some rivers in North America also. The sanctified water is used to cleanse hands in a symbolic gesture of cleaning body and mind.

Vara Puja

Dialogue between the bride's father and the groom.

Following the opening mantras to consecrate the water and offer prayers to a variety of Hindu gods, the bride's father declares his intention to give his daughter in marriage at this auspicious time, in this location (*sankalpam*). He then welcomes the groom, and makes the offer of his daughter's hand in marriage. The groom acknowledges, and agrees to perform the wedding rites to become a householder, to the best of his knowledge.

- **Jayamala/Jai Mala**: Exchange of garlands.

The bride arrives escorted by her maternal uncle(s), and/or aunts, sisters, cousins and friends and/or bridesmaids.

At this stage some families raise a screen or **Antarpat** (see below) to block the groom's view of her approach. Rice or a mixture of sweet and bitter materials (**Jeeriga Bellum**, a mixture of cumin and brown sugar) may be tossed over the screen by both before the screen is lowered.

Hasta Milap

The bride garlands the groom, and is, in turn, garlanded by him. The bride's father (or stand-in) joins their right hands.

- **Pravara**: Announcement of lineage. A formal public announcement of the names of the bridegroom and the bride now follows in front of the assembled. In some traditions this step takes place earlier with some elaboration at the Swagatam when the Barat arrives. The principals are announced by declaring their lineage beginning with great-grandfather and proceeding with grandfather and father from both families. This serves as an opportunity to remember the ancestors on this auspicious occasion and seek their blessing. Traditionally the Pravara is recited three times, but can be done just once.

- **Kanyadanam**: Giving away the bride.

The bride's father repeats his intention to offer his daughter in marriage. The bride and groom face each other with the bride's cupped palms above the groom's, supporting the bride's father's cupped palms holding a coconut. Some families may have a slightly different arrangement of palms. The bride's mother pours consecrated water from a kalasha (traditional water urn) over the coconut while the priest or the bride's father chants mantras for the wellbeing of the bride in her new life.

Note also: a child may be selected to collect the water poured so the audience has a clear view!

- **Mangalyadharanam**: Tying the mangalasutra.

The *māngalyam* placed on a plate and sprinkled with flowers and akshata is taken to the front row to have it blessed by elders of both families.

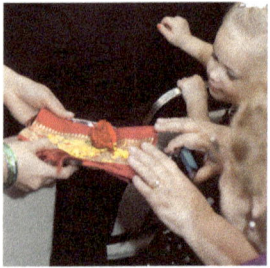
māngalyam being blessed by elders

While the tying of the mangalasutra necklace around the bride's neck is very traditional to South Indian custom, it is common enough to other parts of India to be included as a basic step. The modern necklace is tied with a clasp or hook but, for the purpose of this ritual, may also be tied with the 3 turmeric-tinted threads, first by the groom, followed by his mother and then by his sister. Some traditions consider this to be the point at which the couple is declared married.

Assisting the tying of the *māngalyam*

Mangalasutra necklace with a clasp

- **Agni/Homas**:

Homa, or **Havan**, the fire ritual, is a crucial step among Hindu wedding rites. In orthodox families, when weddings were performed in a village in the bride's home,

the fire from the bride's family's own domestic fire was kindled by the priest or by the groom and, in some cases would be preserved to accompany the bride to her new home. The fire god, Agni, is considered to be not only the recipient of worship here, but also as the priest and a witness acting as an intercedent between the new couple and the gods to whom the incense from offerings made into the havan kund ascends. During these first rituals (**Pradhana Homa**) the couple makes offerings of *sāmagris*: ghee (clarified butter), grain, herbs, incense, sandalwood and/or a spice mixture, declaring that all their material possessions are indeed those of Agni and other gods invoked.

- **Mangal Phera**: Circling the fire. This rite is also called **Laja Homa**.

The bridegroom holds the right hand of the bride while together they walk four times, sunwise, around the *agni kunda* (fire vessel) with garments knotted together (**Gatha Bandan**). The four rounds, or circumambulations are dedicated to the ideal of *chaturvidha phala purushārtha*, by which two vital aspects of life, *artha* (material) and *kāma* (emotional), are controlled by *dharma* (right conduct) in order to achieve *moksha* (salvation).

The groom leads the bride for three rounds, sunwise, as he or the priest chants the mantras. The fourth round, however, praying for moksha, is led by the bride. As they return to the starting point, after each round, they offer *lāja* (puffed rice) to Agni. While a variety of puja materials (*havan sāmagri*) are offered in the primary fire ritual, during **Laja Homa** only *lāja* (parched/puffed rice) is offered. The bride's brother (or a friend) stands to one side at the head of the kunda with a bowl of parched/puffed rice and fills the open palms of the bride with it at the end of each round. As the mantras are chanted by the groom or the priest in his behalf, the bride offers the contents to the fire while the groom offers a spoonful of *lāja* or ghee.

At the end of the fourth round, in some families, *sindhoor* is appled to the bride's parting at the hair and the bride may be asked to place her foot on a stone slab (**Ashmarohana**), symbolizing stability after which th1.1503 ine groom may place toe rings on the second toe of each foot.

She may also, at this point, also be directed to view the Pole Star (**Dhruva Darshan**), or the star Arundhati, symbols of stability or fidelity.

A number of family-based extra customary rites can be added here. These include: vows; ritual gifts of clothing and jewelry, especially bangles; rites to ward off adverse events; rites involving games of tossing of rice, e.g. *Talambrālu* (an Andhra custom in which copious amounts of rice are poured by both on each other's heads, or flower petals); an *ārati*; and special blessings for the bride by married women: "***Saubhagyavati Bhava***" (May you be fortune-favored).

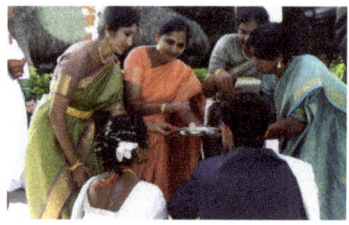 

ārati   *Talambrālu*

- **Saptapadi**: Seven Steps.

Indian civil law recognizes the completion of the seven steps to be the climax of the ceremony and the finalization of the act of marriage. Each step specifies a separate blessing, for food, strength, fidelity, love, welfare of cattle (health), prosperity, and sacred illumination.

Even this basic rite has different versions. One version prescribes that seven circles be drawn using rice flour to the north of the *agni kunda* and that the couple step into each circle holding hands, led by the bridegroom as the latter chants the appropriate verses. Again, the circles may be heaps of raw rice, or, in yet another version, seven lines are drawn in one large circle of rice and the bride places her right foot on one line after another. In some cases, as the groom recites the mantras, he bends down to hold, with his right hand, the right large toe of the bride to help her take each step. At each step he prays that Mahavishnu follow and bless the bride and grant the wishes stipulated in that step. Some parents recall circling the fire seven times. The confusion may be due to a *shloka* (verse) which refers to circles (*mandala*) which is intended to refer to the circles into which the bride and the groom step.

The most popular and acceptable choice is for the bride and groom to take the seven steps together, holding hands, in one circumambulation around the fire.

- **Ashirvadam**: Blessings.

Note: Bent heads during blessing

In this concluding step, seven chants of blessings are invoked for the couple as they stand together, in the names of many divine and legendary couples, as the audience chants *tathastu*, "It shall be so" and sprinkles *akshata* (turmeric-tinted rice) on their heads. They may also seek blessings from elders in the family following this final step. The ceremony is complete with the priest declaring the couple as the newly wedded Mr. and Mrs. ….

And the ceremony ends!

We wish you the very best on your special day and bless you with long, healthy and prosperous life as husband and wife. May God bless you!

Frequently Asked Questions

General Questions

1. How do we select the date/time for the ceremony?

Good question. In India, for a few centuries now, many families have consulted their elders, family priest and astrologer and, using the horoscopes of the bride and the groom, a date and time (*muhurt, muhurtam*) are selected and are strictly abided. Parents pay particular attention that the climactic event (for example, tying of the *mangalasutra*) does indeed occur during the specific time interval chosen apriori and announced in invitations. This is what most people know or remember when they consider the question now.

Here in North America, our experience has been that, more often than not, a date is chosen after the couples determine the date/s of availability of their most favorite location (a beautiful spot they saw on their vacation, a beach, a mansion, a hotel, etc.). Then the parents are informed and the priest is informed at the very end of the process!

Even in India, the choice of date/time may be driven by family traditions which do vary very considerably. For example, New Moon day (*Amavāsya*) is avoided by many families whereas it is preferred by some! Go figure!

Generally, even when the couples come to us with a date already frozen, and if they inquire about the "proper" time, we suggest avoiding the inauspicious *Rāhukālam* for the ceremonial part of the wedding. Even here some priests will tell you that *Rāhukālam* avoidance is relevant only for travels!

So all we can tell you is to follow the family practice and you will be fine.

2. How long should the ceremony be?

Normally, our basic format requires no more than an hour. Extra family options may require additional time.

3. What are the most essential steps?

It depends. First review your family traditions. What have they followed? What motivates the question? Time? Audience?

Briefly the essential steps may be stated: Greeting the groom and family (Swāgatam), declaration of intentions (Sankalpam), Jayamāla, Kanyādānam, Māngalyadhāranam, Homās and Saptapadi. Our experience is that both Hindus and non-Hindus appreciate the brevity, thoroughness and relevance of the steps we have defined.

4. Do we have to take our shoes off before we get on the mantap?

Yes, you do. A mantap is sacred ground when once it gets sanctified with ritual prayers and waters from the invoked sacred rivers. In fact even in the Bible you find reference to this when God is said to have mandated it to Moses:

> *Then the Lord said to him, Remove the sandals from your feet, for the place where you are standing is holy ground and worthy of veneration.*

This is an ancient practice which crosses cultures and is retained by some cultures even now. So we recommend that you do take your shoes off when you are at/on the mantap.

5. Can we substitute candles in place of actual fire?

Agni, the god of fire, is invoked using the Rig Veda mantra (I, 1.1). As such the invoked fire has to have certain features defined as number of tongues, etc. Thus it is highly recommended that actual fire (flame) be used except under special circumstances where it is not practical to do so. Note that the total time the fire container (agni kunda, havan kund) needs to be on the mantap in our format is only about ten to fifteen minutes.

6. Are there seven steps or seven rounds around the fire?

Seven steps. Sapta means seven and padi refers to steps. The reference books discuss minor variations on this principal theme.

7. Can we use English instead of Sanskrit?

For personal vows and interfaith passages English is suitable. All the mantras are in Sanskrit and have been reverentially used in ceremonies over many centuries. English translations of major steps can be used to illustrate a program note.

8. Bride: Can I wear white? Groom: Can I wear a tuxedo for the ceremony?

Yes, you can if you feel the need and/or feel more comfortable. Otherwise the reception may be the more suitable venue for Western wear. Brides in white need to consider the common use of akshata (turmeric-tinted rice) during blessings as well as the fact that they will be circling a fire in what is often a narrow space.

9. Do we have to prostrate to seek blessings of parents, priest and elders in the families?

Not if you feel awkward or uncomfortable. But if that IS the tradition in your family, this is one of the few times in your life in the West when you will get this special blessing at an opportune moment. In this format, it comes at the very end of the ceremony before you walk down the aisle.

10. Can a relative perform the wedding? What about the legality aspect?

Yes, indeed, if he/she is knowledgeable in the Sanskrit mantras and the procedures. In so far as the legality is concerned, if the town where you obtained the marriage license formally recognizes the credentials of the priest, then he/she can sign the marriage certificate. Otherwise, it is best to go to the town hall and go through a brief civil ceremony and have it recorded. You may also need to verify state requirements concerning priests.

11. Is it OK to serve meat at the reception?

Yes. The restrictions are relevant to the sacred space (mantap) and the ceremony only.

Specific Questions by Principals

12. Bride: what do I need to say or do, and when?

As bride, your main role is to look your best on your special day! You will not be speaking unless you and your groom choose to exchange vows.

You will enter the scene, usually after the Vara Puja, and approach the mantap either carrying a garland or receiving it from your chief bridesmaid/maid of honor and proceed to garland the groom.

If your ceremony includes the Antarpat rite, and Jeeraga-Bellum, then you may toss a bitter-sweet mixture over the curtain before the Jayamāla (Garland Exchange).

During the Kanyādānam, you will cup your palms placed above your groom's cupped palms and below your father's palms, for the ceremony. A coconut will rest on the father's palms.

During the first part of the ceremony you will stand next to your parents; after Māngalya Dhāranam, you will be instructed to move next to the groom and his parents, to his left.

During Lāja Homa, you will hold each other by the right hand and circle the fire with the groom leading three times and you leading him the last and fourth time. After each round, you will both offer lāja (parched rice) into the fire. During the previous Pradhāna Homa, the groom makes the offerings. Here you are the primary offerant, although he may participate also.

If the Ashmārohana rite is included, you will place your right foot on a stone slab while the priest charges you to be constant. This follows Lāja Homa and is also the right moment for the groom to place toe-rings on your feet, if it is the family practice.

For Saptapadi, you and your groom will circle the fire, stepping together, holding right hands.

13. Groom: what do I need to say or do, and when?

As groom, you do have words to speak, a few or more, according to your ability with Sanskrit.

Following the Kanyādānam rite, you are the chief performer, taking on that role from the bride's father.

Following the Barāt, you, your parents, relatives and friends will go to meet the bride's parents and friends, led by the priest, waiting at an appointed place. A small ceremony of greeting, Swāgatam or Milni, will take place. The bride's mother will perform an ārati, the bride's father or appointed relative will garland you, the priest will bless you, and you will be led to the mantap.

At the mantap, after an appropriate introduction, prayer, and sanctification, you will be welcomed and honored (Vara Puja). This consists of a short dialogue in Sanskrit.

After the dialogue, the bride is led in. She will garland you first at the mantap and then you will garland her (with the garland you were wearing).

The bride's father will place her right hand in your right hand (Hasta Milāp).

Your ancestry and the bride's are recited (Pravara) by the priest, followed by the bride's father's announcement of his purpose to give you his daughter.

For the Kanyadānam rite, see the description for the bride, above.

Māngalya Dhāranam: with the help of the priest you perform a brief worship of the mangalasutra which has just been blessed by the elders in both families. Then with the help of your mother and sister, you tie or clasp the necklace around the bride's neck. You may apply a touch of sindhoor to the bride's forehead at the hair parting. You may also have a Ring Exchange and/or exchange Vows at this time.

Pradhāna Homa: after the fire is kindled and presented, and invoked by the priest, you will make several offerings into the fire while you and/or the priest chant the mantras. You are establishing your new domestic hearth. Your garment will then be knotted to the bride's by parents (Gatha Bandana).

Lāja Homa: you will lead the bride 3 times around the fire; she will lead you the fourth time. Following each circle she (and you) will offer lāja (poured into your palms by the bride's brother).

At the end of the fourth round is when you may apply toe-rings to the bride's feet, set on a slab (the second toes).

Saptapadi: Holding the bride's right hand, you step together, taking 7 steps, with the priest reciting a mantra at each stop. You may also recite, especially the last mantra, in Sanskrit and/or English. After this the ceremony is essentially over except for blessings you receive.

14. As bride's father, what do I need to say or do, and when?

As bride's father, you are the chief performer of the ceremony until the groom takes over after Kanyādānam. You go with your family and the priest to meet the groom at Swāgatam/ Milni. You wait at the appointed place for the Barāt party and groom to approach. Your wife performs an ārati, the priest blesses, and you garland the groom. You then lead him back to the mantap.

Vara Puja: Following introduction, prayers and purification rites, you will welcome the groom with a short dialogue in Sanskrit. The bride is led in, escorted by maternal uncles or by bridesmaids or friends. She garlands the groom and is garlanded by him.

Hasta Milāp: You place her right hand in his.

Kanyādānam: You make a statement of intent to offer your daughter as bride to this young man, and offer blessings and hope for her future with him. You hold a coconut in your cupped palms, the bride's cupped palms are below yours, the groom's below her palm. While the priest (or you) chants the mantras, your wife pours sanctified water over the coconut and assembled palms.

From this point on, your role will be one of offering blessings with akshata when called on by the priest.

15. As bride's mother, what do I need to say or do, and when?

As bride's mother, you have had a primary role in the multitude of preparations leading up to this wedding day. As the ceremony begins, you will go with your family and the priest to meet the groom at Swāgatam/ Milni. You will be accompanied by at least 5 ladies with assorted thalis of fruits, flowers, decorated coconut, perfume, etc. You wait at the appointed place for the Barāt party and groom to approach. You perform an ārati, the priest blesses, and your husband garlands the groom. You then lead the groom back to the mantap.

At the mantap, the various plates of material will be placed on tables and off one side to be available when needed. Following an introduction and prayers, there will be a water purification rite in which you may be asked to pour water into a kalasha for use in the ceremony.

Following the Vara Puja, your daughter will arrive to garland the groom at the mantap. If there is an Antarpat/and/or Jeeraga-Bellum rite you will need to help her handle the material. After the declaration of intent made by the bride's father, you will follow the direction of the priest and pour water over the coconut on the assembled palms during the Kanyadānam rite.

Mangalyadhāraṇam: it will be helpful if you receive the mangalasutra and rings which have been blessed by elders, and keep them ready for use.

For the Homas, you need to keep the sāmagri for Pradhāna and lāja for Lāja Homa handy for use. Also the couple needs to be knotted together or tied together with a ceremonial cord (which shouldn't get in their way during the rites). Akshata and/or petals should also be kept handy for blessings. Other than these housewifely duties, of course you need to smile and enjoy the event!

With the right group of helpers and a rehearsal, much of the off-stage concerns can be handled by others.

16. As groom's mother, what do I need to say or do, and when?

On the day itself, there is not much needed apart from your gracious presence. You will be greeted at the Swāgatam/Milni and escorted to the mantap. There your main role will be to help the groom tie or clasp the mangalasutra around the bride's neck. You can also help with the knotting or tying of the garments and, of course, many blessings.

17. As groom's father, what do I need to say or do, and when?

As groom's father, you will be greeted, along with your wife, relatives and friends at the Swāgatam/Milni location and escorted to the mantap. Your gracious presence and blessings are essential for the ceremony to be complete.

This book accompanies an audiobook as well as an ebook version which you may purchase separately. And you may also consider buying a CD from CD Baby which contains all the mantras chanted in the exact order shown in my book.

Good luck and best wishes.

Also by Dr. A.V. Srinivasan

Dr. A.V. (Sheenu) Srinivasan, long term U.S. resident, award-winning author, and director of the Vedic Institute of Connecticut, is a popular speaker on Hinduism with appearances in many venues: college campuses, libraries, churches and temples, and yoga and community centers. Best known for the Vedic (Hindu) and interfaith weddings he has conducted nationwide, he is also author of ***Hinduism for Dummies***.

Dr. A. V. Srinivasan, Genre: Spirituality, Hinduism, Hindu Scriptures www.avsrinivasan.com, http://www.youtube.com/watch?v=4tfJbxmBMYo and http://youtu.be/b8L1kJT9xZU 860-633-0045; manager@periplusbooks.com

Puranas: A Magnifying Glass for Vedic Wisdom

Available as an ebook on Amazon and other outlets.

In this excellent work on the *Purāṇas*, Dr. Srinivasan has again made the highly complex and sophisticated literature of an equally complex and sophisticated culture accessible to the contemporary reader.

"Dr. Srinivasan has a gift for communicating complex ideas in a way that makes them clear and easy to grasp, ..."—Professor Jeffery Long, Elizabethtown College, PA

The Bhagavad Gita: A Thread through the Eighteen Gems—A Re-reading

A re-reading of the Hindu classic, the **Bhagavad Gita**, a dialogue between Prince Arjuna and his charioteer Lord Krishna. This occurs in the Sanskrit epic, The Mahabharata, and is often read for its own sake and given the status of scripture by Hindus. ISBN: 978-0-978-5443-6-2

'*This is a brilliant book, …*'—Professor Subhash Kak, Oklahoma State University, OK

"*Srinivasan's commentary is itself a gem. It combines an accessible, easy style of writing with a rigorous translation… It can serve both as a guide for beginners and a springboard for conversation and reflection for advanced practitioners…*"— Professor Jeffery Long

A Hindu Primer: Yaksha Prashna

Third, enlarged, edition. A valuable introduction to Sanskrit Retelling of the Mahabharata episode of the Questions of the Yaksha in the Aranya Parva. Translation and transliteration into English from the original Sanskrit; includes Sanskrit script—86 pages. Foreword by Professor Peter M. Scharf. Non-sectarian Hindu values are imparted through a series of riddles. ISBN: 978-0-9785443-5-5 *** The ebook edition is winner of the IBPA's **Benjamin Franklin Digital Silver Award, 2016** ***

"Dr. Srinivasanji has rendered a great and noble service in bringing forth this beautiful publication. He has given Hindu parents a wonderful and valuable tool that will help instill qualities essential for successful living."—Swami Satchidananda

THE VEDIC WEDDING: Origins, Tradition & Practice

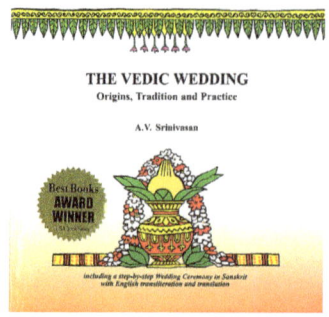

Includes a step-by-step wedding ceremony in Sanskrit, with English transliteration & translation; ISBN 13: 978-0-9785443-0-7 Hard Cover; Illustrations by Bapu; Color photographs.

HINDU WEDDING: The Guide
ISBN 978-1-935052-38-8 paperback

CHANTINGS FOR A HINDU WEDDING CEREMONY [CD]

"I am truly blown away not only by its lucidity and relevance but also by the lovely illustrations that adorn its pages. I have read only about twenty pages and that is only because I revisited each page numerous times."—Dr. Shyam Krishnamurthy, Yale University

"It will be immensely valuable to Hindus in America.... It will be equally important to scholars who study living Hinduism, and to all who are interested in cross-cultural wedding traditions."— Dr. Karen Anderson, Assistant Dean, Wesleyan University

Hinduism for Dummies

Your hands-on guide to one of the world's major religions

The dominant religion of India, "Hinduism" refers to a wide variety of religious traditions and philosophies that have developed over thousands of years. Today, the United States is home to over two million Hindus.

If you've heard of this ancient religion and are looking for a reference that explains the intricacies of the customs, practices, and teachings of this ancient spiritual system, *Hinduism For Dummies* is for you!

"This is a splendid book and I recommend it to anyone seeking a basic knowledge of the world's oldest living faith."—The Rev. Dr. Richard H. Schmidt, November 25, 2013

"Kick me I am new. I had trouble putting this book down! Awesome for someone who knows nothing. Easy to follow and read."—Rev. Kenny October 3, 2014

"I read it in one breath (sorry if this is not a correct English expression). A very complete intro to the whole religion and also a good reference guide. I especially appreciate Mr. Srinivasan's respectful attitude towards every religion."—Martien van Wanrooij, June 30, 2014

HOW TO CONDUCT PUJA

A series of nine individual booklets on HOW TO CONDUCT PUJA to the following gods and goddesses: Soorya, Shiva, SriRamachandra, SriKrishna, MahaaGanapati, Durgadevi, Saraswati, Mahalakshmi and The Navagrahas (1999–2016)

"…*to the point and easy to understand for those learning how to conduct worship…" (Re: Krishna)*—Amazon Customer November 5, 2014

"*The ritual literally allows you to harness the power of these awesome planetary angels to be able to help solve many of the problems in your life". (Re: Navagrahas)*—Amazon Customer March 15, 2013

HOW TO CONDUCT SEEMANTAM

Hindu Rites for the Health of the Mother-to-be

"Very concise, understandable, nicely arranged, informative and complete. Easy to follow."—Krushnakant Shah. January 14, 2014

Speaker Topics

- Dharma: The single most important word in the Hindu lexicon
- Yaksha Prashna: A Compelling Episode in the Mahabharata
- Hindu Temples: History, Sacred Architecture, Rites
- The Hindu wedding ceremony—The Vedic Basis
- Hinduism: A bright thread in the American mosaic

Acknowledgements

I thank my wife Kamla, editor, for patiently reviewing the drafts and making valuable suggestions and comments. Thanks go to the couples whose weddings I have performed as can be seen in the photographs in this book. Very special thanks go to artist Bapu Ramana of Chennai.

www.ingramcontent.com/pod-product-compliance
Ingram Content Group UK Ltd.
Pitfield, Milton Keynes, MK11 3LW, UK
UKHW061223180426
11947UKWH00027B/1995